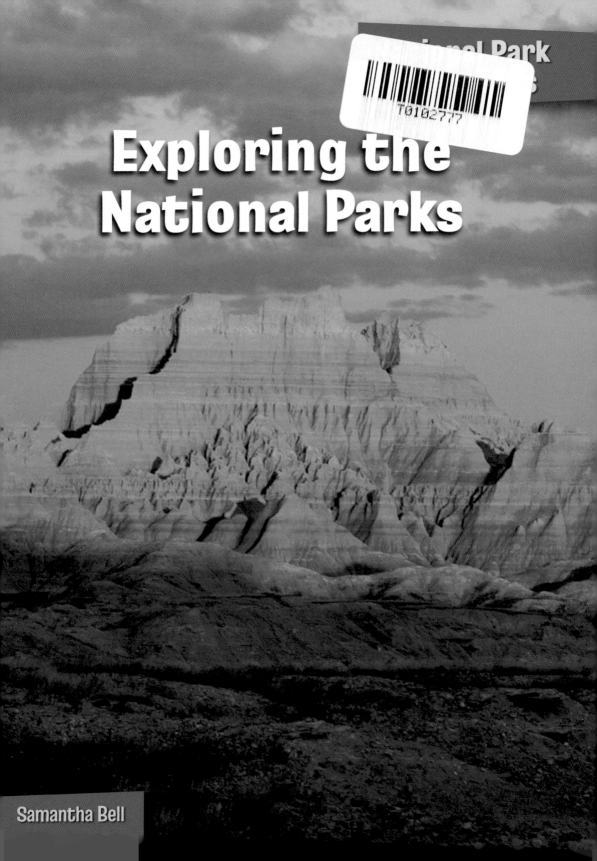

Exploring the National Parks

Samantha Bell

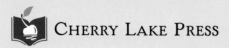

CHERRY LAKE PRESS

Published in the United States of America by Cherry Lake Publishing Group
Ann Arbor, Michigan
www.cherrylakepublishing.com

Reading Adviser: Beth Walker Gambro, MS, Ed., Reading Consultant, Yorkville, IL

Photo Credits: cover, title page: © NPS Photo/Mackenzie Reed; page 4: © Lyle Dorman/Shutterstock; page 5:
© Mark Van Scyoc/Shutterstock; page 7: © orxy/Shutterstock; page 8: © Gray Moeller/Shutterstock; page 11:
National Portrait Gallery, Smithsonian Institution; transfer from the Smithsonian American Art Museum; gift of
Miss May C. Kinney, Ernest C. Kinney and Bradford Wickes, 1945; page 13: Great Falls of the Yellowstone /
W.H. Jackson, photo, Library of Congress Prints and Photographs Division, Washington, DC; page 14: Sitting Bull /
D.F. Barry, photographer, Bismarck, D.T., Library of Congress Prints and Photographs Division, Washington, DC;
page 15: © Machmarsky/Shutterstock; page 17: NPS Photo; page 18: NPS Photo; page 19: NPS Photo; page 21:
NPS Photo; page 22: © Fotos593/Shutterstock; page 23: NPS Photo/Veroncia Verdin; page 24: NPS Photo/C. Aldrich;
page 25: NPS Photo/Jonathan Shafer; page 27: © Image Source Trading Ltd/Shutterstock; page 29: NPS Photo

Cherry Lake Press is an imprint of Cherry Lake Publishing Group.

Library of Congress Cataloging-in-Publication Data

Names: Bell, Samantha, author.
Title: Exploring the national parks / written by Samantha Bell.
Description: Ann Arbor, Michigan : Cherry Lake Publishing, [2024] | Series: National park adventures | Audience:
    Grades 4-6 | Summary: "Welcome to our national parks! Find out what awaits visitors as they explore the vast
    wild spaces of our nation. This title introduces readers to the history of national parks and the many services,
    activities, and people they can find there. Part of our 21st Century Skills Library, this series introduces concepts
    of natural sciences and social studies centered around a sense of adventure"— Provided by publisher.
Identifiers: LCCN 2023010565 | ISBN 9781668927380 (hardcover) | ISBN 9781668928431 (paperback) |
    ISBN 9781668929902 (ebook) | ISBN 9781668931387 (pdf)
Subjects: LCSH: National parks and reserves—United States—Juvenile literature.
Classification: LCC E160 .B45 2024 | DDC 363.6/80973—dc23/eng/20230307
LC record available at https://lccn.loc.gov/2023010565

Cherry Lake Publishing Group would like to acknowledge the work of the Partnership for 21st Century Learning,
a Network of Battelle for Kids. Please visit http://www.battelleforkids.org/networks/p21 for more information.

Printed in the United States of America
Corporate Graphics

Note from publisher: Websites change regularly, and their future contents are outside of our control.
Supervise children when conducting any recommended online searches for extended learning opportunities.

Samantha Bell was born and raised near Orlando, Florida. She grew up in a family of
eight kids and all kinds of pets, including goats, chickens, cats, dogs, rabbits, horses,
parakeets, hamsters, guinea pigs, a monkey, a raccoon, and a coatimundi. She now
lives with her family in the foothills of the Blue Ridge Mountains, where she enjoys hiking,
painting, and snuggling with their cats Pocket, Pebble, and Mr. Tree-Tree Triggers.

CONTENTS

Introduction

National parks are a place to discover the wonders of the natural world. The United States created the first national park in 1872. Since then, other governments have created national parks. Today, there are national parks in over 100 countries. In 1983, historian Wallace Stegner wrote about the national parks. He called them "the best idea we ever had."

CHAPTER 1

What Is a National Park?

National parks are some of the most scenic and historic places in the United States. These areas are set aside by the **federal** government for people to enjoy. The parks help preserve the land, wildlife, and cultural **resources** of an area. In the parks, these things are left alone as much as possible. That way, visitors can really experience them. Visitors might go sightseeing. They may try outdoor activities such as hiking, camping, or climbing. In a national park, there are always new things to explore.

National Park sites can be found in every U.S. state and in Washington, D.C. They are also in the U.S. possessions of Guam, Puerto Rico, American Samoa, and the Virgin Islands.

Court of the Patriarchs in Zion National Park in Utah

The Kuskulana River can be found in Wrangell-St. Elias National Park and Preserve.

Together, they cover more than 85 million acres (34 million hectares). Alaska contains 55 million acres (22 million ha) of these park lands.

Individuals purchased some of the sites. Then they gave them to the country so everyone could visit. The U.S. government purchased other areas. The largest national park site is Wrangell-St. Elias National Park and Preserve in Alaska. It covers 13.2 million acres (5 million ha). The smallest site is the Thaddeus Kosciuszko National Memorial in Pennsylvania. It is 0.02 acres (.008 ha) in size.

The United States and its possessions have 424 national park sites. Sixty-three of these sites are actual national parks. In these parks, the land and water are left in their natural state. Some places are even off-limits to visitors because resources in the area are very fragile. They need extra protection. They could be cultural **artifacts**, such as cave paintings. They may be endangered plants or animals. Another kind of national park site is a national monument. These sites preserve a single natural or cultural resource. They often include special landforms or historic structures. National park sites also include historic parks and national memorials. These were created to remember important people, places, and events in U.S. history. Other national park sites are waterways, scenic trails, and recreation areas.

A VOICE FOR NATIVE AMERICANS

A cabinet secretary is an official who oversees a government department. Cabinet secretaries also advise the U.S. president about matters within their department. The secretary of the interior manages the country's public lands. These include the national parks. The secretary is also responsible for relations between the U.S. government and Native American tribes. In 2021, Deb Haaland became the secretary of the interior. She is a member of New Mexico's Laguna Pueblo group. She is the first Native American to serve as a cabinet secretary. She understands the needs of Native people and their communities.

CHAPTER 2

How the National Parks Got Their Start

The idea of creating a national park began with the American West. In the 1800s, more and more settlers began moving westward. The West's vast, beautiful landscapes inspired artists and writers. Scientists also wanted to explore the land. But many of them were worried. They thought that as more people moved in, much of the natural beauty would be lost. Artist George Catlin devoted his life to painting Native Americans in their homelands. In 1832, Catlin headed to the Great Plains. He wanted to paint the tribal groups that were already disappearing. During the trip, he wrote a note calling

Artist George Catlin is credited for coming up with the idea of national parks.

for the government to create a national park. He wanted a place where the people, animals, and wilderness would be protected.

At first, Catlin's idea did not lead to any changes. But in the years that followed, the government began protecting individual sites. Then in 1871, Congress appointed Ferdinand Hayden to lead a fact-finding mission around the Yellowstone River. This river flows through Wyoming and Montana. Hayden took a team of scientists with him. When the group returned, Hayden also supported the creation of a national park. He convinced Congress to act on the idea. In 1872, Yellowstone became the first national park. During the next 40 years, the U.S. government established more national parks and monuments. At first, various government agencies managed these areas. In 1916, President Woodrow Wilson signed an act creating the National Park Service. This new department would eventually oversee all national parks and monuments. It would also manage historic and recreational areas.

The Lower Falls of the Yellowstone River

Sitting Bull was a Hunkpapa Lakota spiritual leader.
He fought the U.S. Army for control of sacred tribal lands.

While the national parks offer so much natural beauty, there is a dark side to their story. As more people moved west, the federal government began forcing Indigenous nations from their homelands. They forced them onto **reservations**. Much of the Indigenous peoples' land became national parks, including their sacred sites. Today, many tribes remain near the parks. They keep their connection to the land. Many even work to get their land back.

LEARNING TO PRESERVE THE LAND

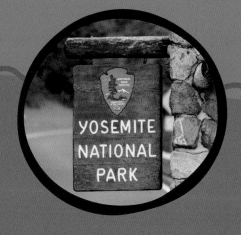

For hundreds of years, Native Americans lived in Yosemite Valley in California. In the mid-1800s, miners, settlers, and tourists came into the region. They damaged the land and its resources. **Conservationists** convinced President Abraham Lincoln that the area needed to be protected. In 1864, Lincoln signed the Yosemite Valley Grant Act. The act gave California the Yosemite Valley and Mariposa Big Tree Grove. The state had to take care of these places so people could visit and enjoy them. It was the first time the government set aside a wilderness area to preserve it. Yosemite became a national park in 1890.

CHAPTER 3

Welcome to the Visitor Center

Every national park has many things to see and do. One of the best places to start is at the visitor center. The visitor center is usually located near the park entrance. Inside, visitors can find all the information they need about the park. People can find maps and trail guides. They can get **brochures** of sights and activities. Many visitor centers also offer special exhibits. These are often about the park and its history. Some visitor centers include museums with artifacts or artwork. Visitor centers have gift shops, too. People can buy souvenirs such as

The visitor center from the North Rim of the Grand Canyon

Flooding from Soda Butte Creek led to a mud slide.

People planning to visit a national park can find a lot of information online. But the information at the visitor center is the most up-to-date. Here, people can find out about unexpected changes or opportunities in the park. For example, part of the park may have to close. The weather may change suddenly. There might be an unexpected animal sighting or natural **phenomenon**, such as a mud slide. With this information, visitors may want to change their plans before they begin exploring.

Some of the larger parks have more than one visitor center. The centers are located in different areas throughout the park. Often, these centers will provide visitors with different information. One may focus on a certain aspect of the park, such as the wildlife or **geology**. Another may focus on the park's cultural history. People can read about the different visitor centers online. That way, they can decide where they want to stop.

STAMP IT!

At visitor centers, people can buy a national park passport book. The books were created in 1986. They are about the size of a regular passport. Inside the book, the parks are organized by region. Some pages have information about the parks. There are also blank pages. Park visitors can take their books to the visitor center. There, they can get a free ink stamp. The stamp is called a cancellation. It shows the name of the park and the date. The stamps help people keep track of the parks they visit.

CHAPTER 4

Meet the Rangers

Park rangers help visitors understand and enjoy the national parks. They perform many jobs. Some rangers work at visitor centers. They welcome visitors and collect any fees. They answer questions about the park. Rangers also help visitors plan their trip. They can help visitors figure out which hikes would be best for them. They may suggest things for people to see and do. Some rangers plan and present educational programs. They may have programs for school groups as well. Many park rangers lead students on hikes or organize other hands-on activities.

National Park Service ranger, Amala Posey, speaks at Grand Canyon National Park.

Rangers are an essential part of the U.S. national parks.

Rangers also work outdoors. Sometimes they keep records of natural occurrences. For example, some rangers track wildlife. Other rangers report on objects they see in the night sky. They mark the hiking trails and make sure the trails are usable. They check them in all kinds of weather. Some parks have hundreds of miles of hiking trails to maintain. Rangers also participate in search and rescue missions. They may be trained in emergency medical services. Some are trained to fight fires.

"EXPLORE, LEARN, AND PROTECT"

The Junior Ranger Program was created to inspire kids to experience the national parks. It is available at almost every park. During their park visit, kids can complete a series of activities. Then they share their answers with the park ranger. They receive a junior ranger badge and certificate. There are also 10 badges that they can earn from home. The program is designed for kids ages 5 to 13. But people of all ages can participate.

Rangers sometimes lead search and rescue missions.

There are law enforcement rangers who help investigate crimes within national parks.

Some rangers are law enforcement rangers. They patrol thousands of acres in the parks. Their job is to protect the natural and cultural resources. They also work to keep visitors safe. They are like other federal law enforcement officers. They can conduct investigations and make arrests. Some law enforcement rangers want to go even further in their careers. They may become special agents. These highly trained rangers work with the Investigative Services Branch of the National Park System. They help investigate serious crimes within national parks. These crimes could involve violence, theft, or illegal drugs.

CHAPTER 5

So Much to Do

When exploring a national park, visitors should bring some necessary supplies. That way, they can stay safe while having fun. The National Park Service has a list of supplies to bring on their website. First on the list are navigation tools. These include a map, compass, and GPS system. They help visitors avoid getting lost in the parks. Visitors should also have a light source, even if they do not plan to be out after dark. These include flashlights, lanterns, and headlamps. Bringing a lightweight tent or tarp is a good idea, too. It can provide shelter in an emergency. Other important equipment includes a first aid kit, a pocketknife, snacks, and water.

Wearing the proper clothing is important, too. At some parks, people are out in the sun for a long time. To avoid sunburns, visitors should bring sunglasses, a hat, and

National park rangers help visitors navigate the national parks.

A BETTER VIEW OF THE MILKY WAY

Light pollution occurs when there is too much artificial light at night. This light may come from businesses, houses, or streetlights. Light pollution prevents people from seeing the natural night sky. But in some national parks, the skies are still very dark. Visitors can see thousands of stars as well as other objects in the galaxy. These parks are called Dark Sky Parks. Many of these parks also offer astronomy programs for people of all ages.

sunscreen. Long pants and long-sleeve shirts also help. In cooler climates, people should bring jackets, hats, and gloves. But at some parks, the weather can change very quickly. Visitors who plan for the most extreme weather— warm or cold—are often the best prepared.

Depending on which park they visit, people can try many kinds of activities. These include hiking, camping, and fishing. People who do not mind tight spaces might want to try **spelunking**. Those who do not mind heights can try rock climbing. Under the water, people can swim or snorkel. On the water, they can canoe, kayak, boat, and paddleboard. Other park activities may include bicycling,

Dark Sky Parks are designated areas far from light pollution and perfect for stargazing.

horseback riding, and wildlife viewing. Many parks also offer special performances. Visitors can listen to live music, see a play, or watch a craft demonstration. With so many things to do, national parks have something for everyone.

Activity

Plan Your Adventure!

There is so much to see and do in the national parks! What activities would you like to try? If you need more ideas, check out the other books in this series.

Place the Date

Chapter 2 mentions some important dates in national park history. You can get a better understanding of this history by creating a timeline of the events. Start with the events from chapter 2. This includes:

1832 – Artist George Catlin calls for the government to create a national park.

1861 – Congress appoints Ferdinand Hayden to lead a fact-finding mission around the Yellowstone River.

1864 – President Abraham Lincoln signs the Yosemite Valley Grant Act.

1872 – Yellowstone becomes the first national park.

1890 – Yosemite becomes a national park.

1916 – The National Park Service is established.

Now add other important events in U.S. history from the same time period. You can choose some from the list below or from your own research. Then write a short paragraph describing what you learned from the timeline.

1803 – The United States purchases the Louisiana Territory from France, opening western lands to settlers.

1811 – General William Henry Harrison defeats the Shawnee leader Tecumseh at the Battle of Tippecanoe.

1830 – President Andrew Jackson signs the Indian Removal Act, leading to the relocation of more than 46,000 Native Americans to land west of the Mississippi River.

1848 – Gold is discovered at Sutter's Mill in California, sparking the California Gold Rush.

1851 – Congress passes the Indian Appropriations Act, creating the Indian reservation system.

1861 – The Civil War begins.

1865 – President Lincoln is assassinated.

1876 – Crazy Horse and Sitting Bull defeat General George Custer at the Battle of Little Bighorn.

1917 – The United States enters World War I.

Learn More

Books

National Geographic Kids. *National Parks Guide U.S.A. Centennial Edition: The Most Amazing Sights, Scenes, and Cool Activities from Coast to Coast!* Washington, DC: National Geographic Kids, 2016.

Payne, Stephanie. *The National Parks: Discover All 62 National Parks of the United States!* New York, NY: DK Publishing, 2020

Siber, Kate. *National Parks of the U.S.A.* London, UK: Wide Eyed Editions, 2018.

Ward, Alexa. *America's National Parks.* Oakland, CA: Lonely Planet, 2019.

On the Web

With an adult, learn more online with these suggested searches.

"10 Junior Ranger Badges You Can Earn from Home." National Park Trust.

"Ask a Ranger: 10 Essentials." National Park Service.

"Junior Ranger Online." National Park Service.

"National Parks." National Geographic Kids.

Glossary

artifacts (AHR-tih-faktz) objects made by humans who lived in an earlier era

brochures (broh-SHURZ) small booklets that contain pictures and information

conservationists (kahn-suhr-VAY-shuhn-ists) people who helps protect Earth's natural resources

federal (FEH-druhl) having to do with the national government

geology (jee-AH-luh-jee) the study of the physical structure of Earth and how it changes over time

phenomenon (fih-NAH-muh-nahn) a rare or significant fact or event

reservations (reh-zuhr-VAY-shuhnz) areas of land set aside by the U.S. government for Native Americans to use

resources (REE-sorss-ez) materials or substances that can be used in a beneficial way

spelunking (spih-LUHN-king) exploring caves

Index